Spotlight on Colorado

FAMOUS COLORADANS

Samuel Bankoff

PowerKiDS press.

NEW YORK

Published in 2016 by The Rosen Publishing Group, Inc.
29 East 21st Street, New York, NY 10010

Editor: Debbie Nevins
Book Design: Iron Cupcake Design

Cataloging-in-Publication Data

Bankoff, Samuel.
Famous Coloradans / by Samuel Bankoff.
p. cm. — (Spotlight on Colorado)
Includes index.
ISBN 978-1-4994-1530-8 (pbk.)
ISBN 978-1-4994-1531-5 (6 pack)
ISBN 978-1-4994-1533-9 (library binding)
1. Colorado — Biography — Juvenile literature. 2. Colorado — History — Juvenile literature. I. Title.
F776.3 B365 2016
978.8'00992—d23

Photo Credits: MPI/Getty Images, cover; Peter Kunasz/Shutterstock.com, 3; Jon Kopaloff/FilmMagic/Getty Images, 4; 360b/Shutterstock.com, 4; Rolls Press/Popperfoto/Getty Images, 5; DFree/Shutterstock.com, 5; Hulton Archive/Getty Images, 6; Jaminnbenji/Shutterstock.com, 7; Unkown/File:Beckwourth indian warrior05.jpg/Wikimedia Commons, 8; Mathew Brady or Levin C. Handy/File:Kit Carson photograph restored.jpg/Wikimedia Commons, 9; Carptrash/File:Kit Carson statue in Trinidad, Colorado.jpg/Wikimedia Commons, 9; Department of the Interior. Office of Indian Affairs. File:Little Raven (Hosa, Young Crow), Head Chief of the Arapaho, three-quarter-length, seated, 1868 - 1874 - NARA - 518894.jpg/Wikimedia Commons, 10; Unknown/File:Arapaho and Cheyenne delegation. May include "LittleRaven" and "Left Hand". NARA 523676.jpg/Wikimedia Commons, 11; Mathew Brady/File:Chief Ouray - Brady-Handy.jpg/Wikimedia Commons, 11; © AP Photo/The Denver Post, 12; Jeffrey Beall/File:Matchless Mine.JPG/Wikimedia Commons, 13; © AP Photo/The Denver Post, 14; Webster, Oshkosh/File:Baby Doe Tabor.jpg/Wikimedia Commons, 15; Everett Historical/Shutterstock.com, 17; Al Fenn/The LIFE Images Collection/Getty Images, 19; Hulton Archive/Getty Images, 20; FPG/Archive Photos/Getty Images, 21; James L. Amos/National Geographic/Getty Images, 22; LC-D418-7173/Library of Congress, 23; W.H. Jackson/The New York Historical Society/Getty Images, 24; LC-D4-13845/Library of Congress, 25; James Montgomery Flagg/File:Uncle Sam (pointing finger).jpg/Wikimedia Commons, 25; Bain News Service/File:Molly brown rescue award titanic.jpg/Wikimedia Commons, 27; MidiMacMan/File:JUSTINA FORD HOUSE 3091 California St.jpg/Wikimedia Commons, 29; Unknown/File:Justina Ford.jpg/Wikimedia Commons, 29LC-USZ62-10273/Library of Congress, 30; Hulton Archive/Getty Images, 33; © AP Photo, 35; Bobby Bank/WireImage, 37; Gijsbert Hanekroot/Redferns/Getty images, 38; Mark Sandten/Bongarts/Getty Images, 40; LEON NEAL/AFP/Getty Images, 41; Focus on Sport/Getty Images, 42; JEFF HAYNES/AFP/Getty Images, 43; STAN HONDA/AFP/Getty Images, 43; Unknown/File:ChinLinSou.jpg/Wikimedia Commons, 44; Lukas skywalker/File:Federico pena.jpg/Wikimedia Commons, 44; Steve Granitz/Contributor/Getty Images, 45.

Manufactured in the United States of America

CPSIA Compliance Information: Batch #BS15PK: For further information contact Rosen Publishing, New York, New York at 1-800-237-9932

Contents

CHAPTER 1

Great People from a Great State

Condoleezza Rice, former U.S. secretary of state

Countless people have made Colorado the great state it is today. Most of them had names we will never know. Their hard work, courage, and spirit didn't make the history books, but their contributions still matter.

These are the people who built the towns and cities, constructed the rails and roads, turned scrubland into farmland, dammed the rivers, mined the mountains, and named the places. They set up businesses and built schools, hospitals, museums, and theaters. They drew maps, established order, made laws, and organized a government. These people took a vast, beautiful

Mountain climber Aron Ralston (b. 1975) was canyoneering in Utah in 2003 when he became trapped by a falling boulder. His right hand was crushed under the rock. After five days, he cut off his arm with a pocket knife in order to survive. Ralston wrote a book about his ordeal, which was made into the movie *127 Hours* in 2010.

Scott Carpenter (1925–2013) was one of the astronauts selected for NASA's Project Mercury, which was the first U.S. human spaceflight program. He was the second American to orbit the Earth and the fourth in space.

wilderness and turned it into an important and productive state.

Among all those forgotten names, faces, and life stories, however, some stand out. The people pictured on these two pages, for example, are all Coloradans. Turn the page for stories of more brave, bold, and colorful folks. All made Colorado history—and some are still making history today!

A SUPER GIRL
Melissa Benoist (b. 1988) of Littleton is an actress and a singer. She played Marley Rose in the TV series *Glee* and went on to star in *Supergirl* (2015).

CHAPTER 2

The Mountain Men

Zebulon Pike, James P. Beckwourth, Kit Carson

Zebulon Pike wasn't exactly a Coloradan, but his name lives on in the state. In 1806, President Thomas Jefferson sent an **expedition** to explore and map the western wilderness. Army Captain Pike and his group traveled through the Southern Rockies in what today is Colorado. He spotted a mountain he called "Highest Peak." He and his men tried to climb it to get a better view of the region. Deep snow prevented it, but the peak was named in his honor.

Zebulon Pike

Pikes Peak is the highest summit of the Southern Front Range of the Rockies. It's one of Colorado's best-known places and has been designated a National Historic Landmark.

The Pike Expedition was the first official U.S. effort to explore the western Great Plains and the Rocky Mountains.

Pikes Peak is officially spelled without the apostrophe that would otherwise be correct in the word "Pike's." Nevertheless, it's common to find it written both ways today.

But whatever happened to Pike himself? Just a few years later, in 1813, Pike died at age 34 in Canada. He was killed fighting in the Battle of York, part of the War of 1812. But that's another story. He is mainly remembered for his courageous, groundbreaking expedition to Colorado and the book he wrote about it.

Another sort of "mountain man" also made his mark on Colorado history. Mountain men were the fur trappers, traders, and explorers who roamed the Rocky Mountain wilderness, particularly between 1820 and 1840.

Zebulon Pike is credited with the first sighting of the mountain peak, but of course, the Indians knew it was there all along. The Arapaho called it *Heey-otoyoo,'* meaning "Long Mountain." Early Spanish explorers had also seen the mountain in the 1700s. They called it *El Capitán*, or "The Leader."

WRANGLE UP SOME FACTS

Today, ten states have a Pike County named for the explorer. Colorado is not one of them. There is, however, a small town named Kit Carson in Colorado's Cheyenne County.

These rugged characters often lived by themselves in the forests, but sometimes worked in groups. They trapped beaver and sold the pelts at various trading posts across the West. Mountain men helped to chart the wilderness area and establish trading relations with the Indians. When settlers arrived a few years later, they found the Colorado territory to be roughly mapped out, which helped them enormously.

Mountain man **James Pierson Beckwourth** (1798–1866) was an African American. He was

An illustration of Beckwourth dressed as an Indian warrior

born a slave in Virginia, but he was freed and moved out West. There he worked as a trapper for the Rocky Mountain Fur Company. For several years, he lived with a band of Crow Indians and married the chief's daughter. Beckwourth lived a colorful and adventurous life. He told his story in a book of his memoirs.

Christopher "Kit" Carson (1809–1868) was a legend in his own time. On the western frontier, he was a mountain man, a trapper, a soldier, a wilderness guide, and an Indian agent. Like many mountain men, he lived among friendly Indians for a while. At other times, though, he fought hostile Indians and protected the pioneers. The American people considered him a great western hero.

Kit Carson

The Fort Carson Army Base in El Paso, Colorado, was named in honor of Kit Carson.

The Weeminuche moved to the Southern Ute Indian Reservation in southwestern Colorado. They named their capital Ignacio in the chief's honor.

CHAPTER 3

The Chiefs

Little Raven, Chief Ignacio, Chief Ouray

The great **influx** of settlers to Colorado in the 1800s changed the native peoples' lives forever. Many Indian leaders guided their people through those years of **turmoil**, including these notable chiefs.

Little Raven (c.1810–1889) was chief of the Southern Arapaho. When the 1859 **gold rush** brought masses of white settlers to his homeland, he welcomed them. He hoped when the newcomers had taken all the yellow metal they needed, that they would leave. Of course, that didn't happen.

Chief Ignacio (1828–1913) was chief of the Weeminuche band—also called the Southern Utes. Over the years, he watched his people's lands shrink as more and more settlers pushed the Ute off their territory. He watched his people starve, deprived of their old hunting grounds.

"I would like to shake hands with the white men, but I am afraid they do not want peace with us."
—Little Raven

When U.S. President Rutherford B. Hayes met Ouray in 1880, he said the chief was "the most intellectual man I've ever conversed with."

The Cheyenne and Arapaho delegation

When Northern Ute bands rose up and fought the U.S. Army in 1879, Ignacio kept his band out of the violence.

Chief Ouray (1833–1880) was the leader of the Ute tribe that lived in western Colorado. He spoke several languages and was greatly respected. He knew fighting the Americans would spell doom for his people and worked hard for peace.

The chiefs travelled to Washington, D.C., on various occasions to hold **peace talks** with the U.S. government. But time and again, the Americans violated the terms of those **treaties**. The government drew up new treaties, always giving the Indians less and less. In the end, these chiefs sadly watched their way of life die.

When Ouray died in 1880, his obituary in *The Denver Tribune* read, "In the death of Ouray, one of the historical characters passes away. He has figured for many years as the greatest Indian of his time... Ouray is in many respects...a remarkable Indian...pure instincts and keen perception. A friend to the white man and protector to the Indians alike."

CHAPTER 4

The Silver King

Horace Tabor

WRANGLE UP SOME FACTS

Horace Tabor lost more than $9 million in less than a year.

Horace Tabor planned to turn Denver into "the Paris of the West."

Horace Tabor was born in Vermont, but he became a big name in Colorado. He moved out West around the time of the gold rush, 1859, and opened a general store in Leadville. Eventually he became the mayor, but that's not what he's remembered for.

In 1879, miners found silver in a Leadville mine that Tabor had **invested** in. The discovery kicked off the Colorado silver boom, and it also made Tabor a rich man. He invested his money in other mines—most famously the Matchless Mine in Leadville.

MATCHLESS MINE

FROM BOOM TO BUST

In 1878, Congress passed a law requiring the U.S. government to buy large amounts of silver each month from the western silver mines. The silver was made into silver dollars. For mine owners like Horace Tabor, the law meant even greater wealth. In 1893, the silver purchase laws were undone, and the silver industry collapsed. That's how Tabor lost his fortune.

The Tabor Grand Opera House in Denver was as big as an entire city block.

Tabor became even richer! People called him the Bonanza King of Leadville and the Silver King. Tabor used his wealth to build banks, opera houses, and other buildings in Leadville and Denver. He started newspapers and got into politics, where he went far as well. He was the richest man in Colorado!

MONEY ISN'T EVERYTHING

Tabor's first wife, Augusta, was uncomfortable with their sudden wealth. She continued to live frugally and dress modestly. Meanwhile, Horace wanted to live it up. Their different reactions to the windfall led to their eventual divorce.

A SAD END

In 1935, Baby Doe was found frozen to death in her shack at age 81.

Tabor divorced his first wife and married a beautiful, much younger woman named Baby Doe. Denver's high society people gasped at the **scandal**, but Baby Doe became a celebrity in her own right. The couple lived extravagantly and had two daughters, named Lillie and Silver Dollar.

Then the story takes a tragic turn. Tabor lost his fortune, and he died in poverty in 1899. Penniless, Baby Doe lived for years in a one-room tool shack on an old mining property in Leadville. Even young Silver Dollar Tabor came to a bad end. Today, their houses, and even the shack, are museums. Their story is a fascinating tale of **boom and bust**—a true Colorado story.

OPERA HOUSE

The Tabor Grand Opera House in Denver, an immense, elegant theater building, was demolished in 1964. The Tabor Opera House in Leadville still stands.

CHAPTER 5

The Cannibal

Alferd Packer

Alfred "Alferd" Packer achieved fame in a way no one would want. In the winter of 1874, he joined a group of **prospectors** on a journey to search for gold in Colorado. On their way, he and his party met with Chief Ouray, the great Ute leader. Ouray advised the men to wait until spring, as harsh winter weather in the mountains would be very dangerous.

Six men, including Packer, ignored the chief and went on anyway. Sure enough, they became hopelessly lost in the San Juan Mountains. The snow became too deep to go any farther, and they ran out of food.

Four months later, Packer came down from the mountains alone. He kept changing his story and finally claimed a member of the party had gone insane and shot the others. Packer

In 1968, students at the University of Colorado Boulder named one of the school's dining halls after Packer. Today, Alferd Packer Restaurant & Grill serves "meals to die for."

Packer was released from jail in 1901. He was widely rumored to have become a vegetarian, but no one knows if it's true.

said he then shot that man in self-defense. Starving, Packer ate that man's flesh until he could find his way out of the mountains. But people were suspicious. **Cannibalism** was repulsive, but it wasn't a crime. However, if he had killed a man for that purpose, that was different. Packer was eventually charged, found guilty, and jailed.

ALFERD PACKER

Today, no one really knows what happened that cruel winter. The strange case remains a mystery.

KNOWLEDGE NUGGET

Packer was originally named Alfred, but according to one story, his name was tattooed on his arm incorrectly as Alferd. After that, Packer used the misspelled version.

Cody named one of his children Kit Carson, after the mountain man he admired. Sadly, the child died at age five.

CHAPTER 6

The Showman

Buffalo Bill Cody

Like Kit Carson, William F. Cody (1846–1917) became a legend in his own time. Like Carson, Cody came to symbolize the spirit of the great American frontier.

Cody grew up on the Great Plains and worked a number of tough jobs in his youth. In 1867, he got a job hunting buffalo, or bison, for the Kansas Pacific Railroad. The animals were used to feed the rail construction crews. By Cody's own count, he killed 4,280 bison in 17 months. His skill as a sharpshooter earned him his nickname, "Buffalo Bill." He also worked as a scout for the U.S. Army and was involved in several battles.

A WILD TIME FOR THE QUEEN

In 1897, Buffalo Bill's Wild West show was invited to England to take part in Queen Victoria's Golden Jubilee celebration. The show was the hit of the festivities. Nobility, commoners, and even Queen Victoria herself were thrilled by the exotic American extravaganza. The show was even said to have improved British and U.S. relations.

WRANGLE UP SOME FACTS

Cody died in 1917. He is buried at the summit of Lookout Mountain near Denver.

Buffalo Bill is shown on this poster for one of his shows.

WANTED

When Bill Cody was 14, he answered an ad for a job as a Pony Express rider. The Pony Express was the main mail and delivery service between Missouri and California. The company advertised for "skinny, expert riders willing to risk death daily." Cody got the job.

Buffalo Bill looks off into the distance with the American and British flags flying behind him.

Cody's real fame came from two sources. A popular author made Bill into a character in one of his book series. In the books, reality mixed with fantasy as the fictitious Buffalo Bill achieved amazing feats on the American frontier. That reputation led Cody into show business. He created a traveling show that was part circus, part historical pageant.

HIGH IN THE SADDLE

The term "cow-boy" was originally meant as an insult to cattle drivers. Buffalo Bill's shows helped change the cowboy's image by demonstrating bronco riding, roping, and other rodeo skills. Eventually, Americans came to view cowboys with great respect and admiration.

Ned Buntline, the writer who popularized Buffalo Bill as a character in a book series, also wrote popular, partly imaginary stories about other larger-than-life western heroes: Daniel Boone, Davy Crockett, and Kit Carson.

Buffalo Bill's Wild West show played for 30 years to audiences throughout the United States and Europe. It featured cowboys, Indians, buffalo, and western heroes—including sharpshooter Annie Oakley. The show was a sensational success and made Cody one of the most famous Americans in the world.

Bill Cody sits with two Native Americans around 1915.

KNOWLEDGE NUGGET

Cody used his fame to support voting rights for women and the fair treatment of American Indians.

Mount Jackson in the Gallatin Range of Yellowstone National Park, in Wyoming, is named in honor of William Henry Jackson.

CHAPTER 7

The Photographer

William Henry Jackson

Without smart phones, computers, or even television, how could 19th-century Americans know what the western frontier looked like? When travelers described astonishing sights like the Grand Canyon, who knew what to believe? New technology was the answer.

Jackson used this camera on his journey out West.

Photography was that new technology. William Henry Jackson (1843–1942) was an American painter and printmaker, and a Civil War veteran. Mainly, though, he is remembered as a photographer, famous for his images of the American West.

Before Jackson photographed it, some people thought Old Faithful, the geyser in what is now Yellowstone National Park, was a myth.

Mules helped carry Jackson's photography equipment.

In 1870, Jackson and several other men went on an expedition for the U.S. government. The men were sent to explore and document the Yellowstone River and Rocky Mountain area. Jackson was the official photographer. In those days, photography equipment was large, bulky, and heavy. It was extremely cumbersome to lug up craggy mountains and across rushing rivers.

Jackson, right, relaxes with another explorer and an American Indian child in the wilderness.

Jackson returned with the first photographs of many legendary western landmarks. His photos helped convince Congress in 1872 to establish Yellowstone National Park, the first U.S. national park.

The Colorado Rockies in a photo by William Henry Jackson.

In Colorado, Jackson was the first to photograph the prehistoric Native American cliff dwellings in Mesa Verde. He opened his own photo gallery in Denver in 1879 and published his photographs as postcards.

In the end, Jackson took some 80,000 photos of the American West—one of the most important photography collections in the world.

William Henry Jackson was a great-great nephew of Samuel Wilson of Troy, N.Y. "Uncle Sam" Wilson is said to have inspired the character that symbolizes the United States—"Uncle Sam." Both share the initials U.S.

CHAPTER 8

The "Unsinkable"

Margaret "Molly" Brown

The great ocean liner, the RMS *Titanic*, sank on its very first voyage on April 15, 1912. It hit an iceberg in the North Atlantic. The ship had been sailing from England to New York City, with many wealthy and important people on board. More than 1,500 of its 2,224 passengers died. The event shocked the world because the *Titanic* had been famously designed to be unsinkable.

One of the survivors was Margaret Brown (1867–1932) of Denver. She and her husband had started out poor in Leadville, but became rich the way so many Coloradans did in the late 1800s—through mining.

The Browns moved to Denver in 1894, and Margaret became involved in a number of worthy causes. Surviving the *Titanic* disaster made Brown a celebrity in Denver. She was much admired for her courageous deeds helping others during the **catastrophe**.

Margaret Brown's story was made into numerous plays and movies. *The Unsinkable Molly Brown* is a musical. It opened on Broadway in 1960 and was made into a movie in 1964.

KNOWLEDGE NUGGET

Margaret Brown's friends called her Maggie. "Molly" was a Hollywood creation.

Margaret Brown presents a trophy to Captain Arthur Henry Rostron for his service in the rescue of the Titanic.

Though she enjoyed her high society life, Brown was a **progressive** and concerned with the problems of poor people. She used her position to promote a variety of **reforms**. During World War I in France, she helped wounded French and American soldiers.

In many ways, "The Unsinkable" Margaret Brown represented the independent spirit of the West.

UNSINKABLE

A gossip columnist in a Denver newspaper was the first to refer to Margaret as "the Unsinkable Mrs. Brown." The nickname stuck.

Elizabeth Blackwell (1821–1910) was the first female doctor in the United States. She earned her M.D. degree in 1849 in Geneva, New York.

CHAPTER 9

The Doctors

Justina Ford and Florence Rena Sabin

In 1899, when **Justina Ford** graduated from medical college in Chicago, she knew she had a tough road ahead of her. The examiner told her, "You've got two strikes against you to begin with. First of all, you're a lady, and second, you're colored*." Ford knew she faced discrimination. African American doctors and women doctors were few. African American women doctors were even less common. In her later years, Ford said, "I fought like a tiger against those things."

Ford moved to Denver in 1902 and opened a private practice in her home. At the time, black people (doctors and patients) were not allowed in many hospitals. Ford took care of people of all races and backgrounds for

*Colored is an old-fashioned word once used to describe people who were not white. Today the word is considered inappropriate and is not used. Today, "woman" is also the preferred term to "lady."

WRANGLE UP SOME FACTS

Dr. Ford's home in Denver was turned into the Black American West Museum and Heritage Center in 1971. One room is devoted to an exhibition of her life and work.

Dr. Ford cared for her patients in this house near Denver's Five Corners.

50 years. She specialized in caring for pregnant women and delivered some 7,000 babies during her career. Her patients loved her and called her "the Lady Doctor."

Dr. Ford was the first African American woman to be licensed as a physician in Colorado. What's more astonishing, in 1950, just two years before she died, she was still the only black woman physician in the state.

In 1985, Ford was admitted to the Colorado Women's Hall of Fame. In 1989, she was named a "Medical Pioneer of Colorado" by the Colorado Medical Society.

Florence Rena Sabin (1871–1953) was a Colorado doctor who lived at the same time as Ford. Like Ford, she was a pioneer in the medical field, though in a different way. She became one of the first women doctors to build a career as a research scientist. She conducted important research on how unborn babies grow and on how the body fights disease.

Sabin was the first woman to accomplish a number of milestones. For example, she was the first woman to hold a full professorship at the **prestigious** Johns Hopkins School of Medicine. She was also the first woman elected to the National Academy of Sciences. In her later years, Sabin worked for the state of Colorado to improve the health of its citizens.

Rebecca Lee Crumpler (1831–1895) was the country's first African American woman doctor. She earned her M.D. in 1864 from Boston University.

KNOWLEDGE NUGGET

In 1951, in honor of Dr. Sabin's 80th birthday, the University of Colorado's Department of Medicine named a building for her—the Florence R. Sabin Building for Research in Cellular Biology.

The University of Colorado Boulder has a large Glenn Miller Archive, or collection, that includes many of Miller's recordings, gold records, and other important items.

CHAPTER 10

The Bandleader

Glenn Miller

Glenn Miller (1904–1944) played trombone in his high school band in Fort Morgan, Colorado. Like many high school guys, he and his friends formed a band and played the coolest music. In 1920, what was cool was a whole new style of dance band music.

Miller entered the University of Colorado Boulder, but dropped out to be a professional musician. By the 1930s, he was a well-known trombonist, but he found even more success as a songwriter and band conductor. As the leader of the Glenn Miller Orchestra, a so-called big band, he created a unique sound. The "swing music" made people want to get up and dance. He made many records and, in 1942, was awarded the first-ever **gold record** for his song "Chattanooga Choo Choo."

"America means freedom and there's no expression of freedom quite so sincere as music."
—Glenn Miller, during World War II

Every summer, the city of Fort Morgan, Colorado, hosts a public event called the Glenn Miller SwingFest.

During World War II (1939–1945), Miller joined the military and created a new Air Force Band. With its upbeat music, the band boosted the **morale** of the troops.

Glenn Miller plays his trombone in 1934.

In December 1944, Miller left England in a small plane to fly to Paris, France, to play for American soldiers there. His plane never arrived. The mystery of what happened to that plane has never been solved. Glenn Miller is remembered today as possibly the greatest bandleader of all time.

Glenn Miller was the best-selling recording artist from 1939 to 1943. Some of his hits include "Moonlight Serenade," "In the Mood," "Pennsylvannia 6-5000," and "Tuxedo Junction."

CHAPTER 11

The Actress

Hattie McDaniel

There was a time when there were very few movie roles available for black actresses. Pretty much the only character part they were considered for was that of the household maid. Hattie McDaniel (1895–1952) of Denver was an actress during those years. She was also a singer, a songwriter, and a comedian. She was the first African American woman to sing on the radio in the United States. McDaniel appeared in more than 300 films, but she is most famous for her performance in one.

Hattie McDaniel was discriminated against even in death. She had wanted to be buried at the Hollywood Cemetery. When she died in 1952, however, the cemetery denied her request because of her skin color. Only white people were allowed to be buried there at that time.

And what a performance it was! McDaniel played Mammy, a slave and house servant, in the 1939 movie, *Gone with the Wind*. She was not the star of the movie, but whenever she was on the screen, she was truly the star of that scene. Audiences agreed. She went on to receive an Academy Award for

In 2010, the black actress Mo'Nique won an Academy Award for her performance in the move *Precious*. On accepting the award, she paid tribute to McDaniel, saying, "I want to thank Miss Hattie McDaniel for enduring all that she had to, so that I would not have to."

Hattie McDaniel, left, accepts her Academy Award from actress Fay Bainter in Los Angeles.

that performance, becoming the first African American to win an Academy Award.

Despite that award, racial attitudes in the United States did not change in time for Hattie McDaniel to realize her full potential. Today, however, she is celebrated as a remarkable woman of great talent and spirit.

KNOWLEDGE NUGGET

The 1940 Academy Awards Ceremony was held in a fancy hotel with a strict whites-only policy. Hattie McDaniel—one of the winners!—was not allowed to sit at the same table with the rest of the cast of *Gone with the Wind*.

CHAPTER 12

The Folk Singers

Judy Collins, John Denver

Judy Collins (b. 1939) was a Denver girl with a beautiful voice. She learned to play the guitar and piano and became a famous singer-songwriter in the 1960s. Folk music was popular at the time, and she became well-known for her versions of many traditional songs, such as "Amazing Grace" and "Turn, Turn, Turn."

Like many folk singers, Collins became interested in political activism. She sang protest songs by the legendary folk singers Woody Guthrie, Pete Seeger, and Bob Dylan.
In the 1960s and 1970s, she worked for civil rights and against the Vietnam War.

Collins was one of a number of extremely successful folk singers of the time. However, her sweet, clear voice stood out as something truly special. As time went on, she wrote more and

Growing up in Denver, Collins studied classical piano with the renowned orchestra conductor Antonia Brico (1902–1989). Born in the Netherlands, Brico lived in Denver from 1942 until the end of her life. In Colorado, she served as the conductor of the Denver Symphony Orchestra and the Boulder Philharmonic Orchestra.

In 1989, Judy Collins wrote the song "The Blizzard" about being stranded in a Colorado snowstorm. Collins calls it "her Colorado song."

more of her own songs. She also broadened her song choices beyond just folk music.

Today, in her later years, Collins still performs around the country and continues to work for causes she believes in.

Some of Judy Collins's best-selling records include "Both Sides Now," and "Send in the Clowns."

John Denver (1943–1997) was not born in Colorado. He didn't grow up there. But he loved Colorado so much that he took the last name "Denver" in place of his actual name, Deutschendorf. In particular, he loved the Rocky Mountains. After he became a popular singer in the 1970s, he bought a home in Aspen.

KNOWLEDGE NUGGET

Over his career, John Denver recorded about 300 songs, of which 200 were his own compositions.

COMING HOME

Some of Denver's other big hits were "Take Me Home, Country Roads," "Sunshine on My Shoulders," and "Annie's Song."

Denver began as a guitar-playing folk singer. Like Judy Collins, he wrote many of his own songs. He is best known for his song, "Rocky Mountain High." Denver recorded it in 1972 and in 2007, the song was adopted as one of the two official state songs of Colorado.

Like other folk singers, Denver devoted himself to activism. He was especially interested in saving the environment and in fighting world hunger. In addition to singing and songwriting, Denver was an avid photographer and skier. He also loved flying airplanes and became a pilot. In 1997, he died when an experimental plane he was flying ran out of fuel and crashed in California. He was 53.

A POET, BUT WE DON'T KNOW IT?

In 1974, Colorado governor John Vanderhoof named John Denver as the state's poet laureate. Colorado no longer recognizes him as such, however.

CHAPTER 13

The Swimmers

Amy Van Dyken, Missy Franklin

Amy Van Dyken (b. 1973) was born in Denver. As a child, she had **asthma** and began swimming as a way to strengthen her lungs. And boy, could she swim! At the 1996 Olympics, she became the first American woman to win four gold medals.

In 2014, Van Dyken crashed an ATV and severed her spinal cord. The injury left her paralyzed from the waist down. Since then,

Since her accident, Van Dyken has created the Amy Van Dyken Foundation to help people with spinal cord injuries. Its followers call themselves "Amy's Army."

Amy Van Dyken in the 1996 Olympics

Amy Van Dyken is married to Tom Rouen, a former football player with the Denver Broncos.

Franklin is a natural-born U.S. citizen. Both of her parents are Canadian citizens, which gives Franklin dual American-Canadian citizenship. However, Franklin represents the United States exclusively in international competition.

she has been fighting to regain the full use of her legs. When she was finally able to stand again on her own in May 2015, she called it the greatest accomplishment of her life.

Missy Franklin (b. 1995) grew up in Centennial, Colorado. She started swimming at age five and was often inspired by Amy Van Dyken. At age 12, she qualified to try out for the 2008 Olympics, though she didn't make the team.

By the time of the 2012 Olympics in London, Franklin did more than just make the team. She won four gold medals and a bronze medal. Then, in 2013, she became the first female swimmer to win six gold medals at the World Championships. She currently holds the world record in the 200-meter backstroke and U.S. records in both the 100-meter and 200-meter backstroke.

Missy Franklin at the 2012 Olympics

Franklin's dad nicknamed her "Missy the Missile."

In 2004, the University of Colorado honored Billups by retiring his jersey (number 4).

CHAPTER 14

The Ball Players

Goose Gossage, John Elway, Chauncey Billups

In baseball, football, and basketball, Coloradans have made their marks. Here are three great athletes.

Richard "Goose" Gossage (b. 1951) is a former Major League Baseball player from Colorado Springs. During his 22-year career, he pitched for nine different teams, including the New York Yankees and the San Diego Padres. He was known for his fastball, which was clocked at 98 to 102 miles per hour in his prime. Gossage was elected to the Baseball of Fame in 2008. He now works in broadcasting.

On August 4, 1994, Gossage became the third pitcher in major league history to appear in 1,000 games.

John Elway (b. 1960) spent his entire football career in Colorado. He was a quarterback for the Denver Broncos from 1984 to 1999. During that time, he led his team to win two Super Bowl titles two years in a row. He came back to the Broncos in 2011 to serve as the team's general manager and a vice president of the organization.

Chauncey Billups (b. 1976) is a native of Denver. He was a hoops star at the University of Colorado Boulder and went on to play pro basketball. He played with the Denver Nuggets from 2008 to 2011, helping them win 50 games two seasons in a row. After a 17-year career, he retired in 2014.

When he was with the Denver Nuggets, Billups chose the number 7 jersey to honor Denver Broncos quarterback John Elway.

Today a stained-glass window portrait of Chin Lin Sou hangs in the Colorado state capitol, commemorating him as Colorado's leading Asian pioneer leader.

CHAPTER 15

So Many More!

Helen Hunt Jackson (1830–1885) was an American poet and writer who spent part of her life in Colorado Springs. She became an activist who worked to improve the treatment of Native Americans by the U.S. government. In her 1881 book, *A Century of Dishonor*, she described the many times the government has broken its treaties with the Indians.

Chin Lin Sou

Chin Lin Sou (1836–1894) immigrated to the United States in 1859 from China to work on constructing the nation's cross-country railroads. He and his family settled in Denver, where he became a successful businessman and community leader. At the time, U.S. law forbade all Chinese from becoming citizens.

Katharine Lee Bates (1859–1929) spent a summer teaching English in Colorado Springs.

Peña Boulevard, a freeway in Denver and Aurora, is named for Federico Peña.

She wrote the song "America the Beautiful" after looking out from the summit of Pikes Peak. "When I saw the view, I felt great joy. All the wonder of America seemed displayed there, with the sea-like expanse."

Federico Peña (b. 1947) became the first Hispanic mayor of Denver in 1983. He was reelected in 1987. During the presidency of Bill Clinton, Peña served as the U.S. secretary of transportation. He went on to become the U.S. secretary of energy from 1997 to 1998.

Temple Grandin (b. 1947) is a professor of animal science at Colorado State University. Being autistic herself, Grandin has written books about and supported the rights of autistic people. She has also worked to raise awareness of animal welfare. The livestock industry has used her insight into the animal mind to improve conditions for cattle.

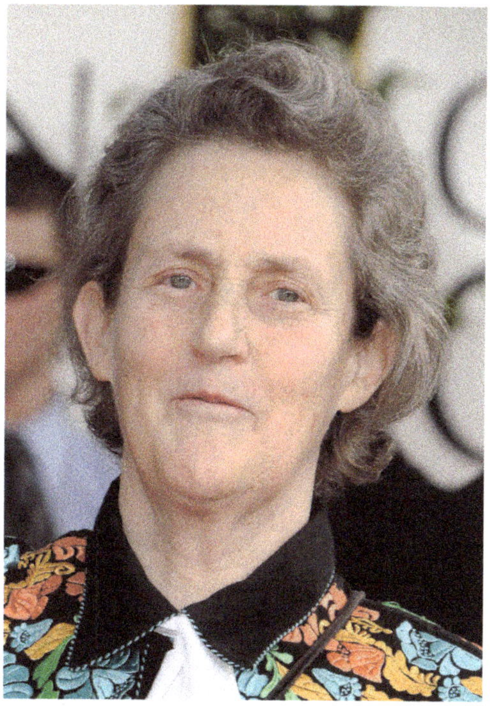

Temple Grandin

Temple Grandin was named one of 2010's 100 most influential people in the world by *Time* magazine.

Glossary

asthma—a lung disease in which a person's airways become swollen, making breathing difficult

boom and bust—a situation in which a period of great prosperity or rapid economic growth (boom) is quickly followed by one of economic decline (bust)

cannibalism—the eating of human flesh by a human being

catastrophe—disaster

expedition—a journey undertaken by a group of people for the purpose of exploration or scientific research

gold record—a gold phonograph record awarded to a singer or group whose single record or album has sold at least 500,000 copies

gold rush—the rapid movement of people to a place where gold has recently been discovered

influx—the arrival of large numbers of people

invest—put money into a scheme or project with the hope of making even more money

morale—the mental or emotional spirits of a person or group; a state of confidence, cheerfulness, and enthusiasm

peace talks—discussions between warring sides aimed at achieving peace

prestigious—highly respected or admired

progressive—forward looking, favoring change or improvement

prospectors—people who are looking for mineral deposits, usually gold

reforms—improvements; changes made in order to make a situation better

scandal—disgrace; an event or behavior that causes public outrage, shock, anger, or gossip

treaty—official written agreement

turmoil—trouble

Index

Due to the changing nature of Internet links, the Rosen Publishing Group, Inc., has developed an online list of websites related to the subject of this book. This site is updated regularly. Please use this link to access the list: http://www.powerkidslinks.com/soco/fc